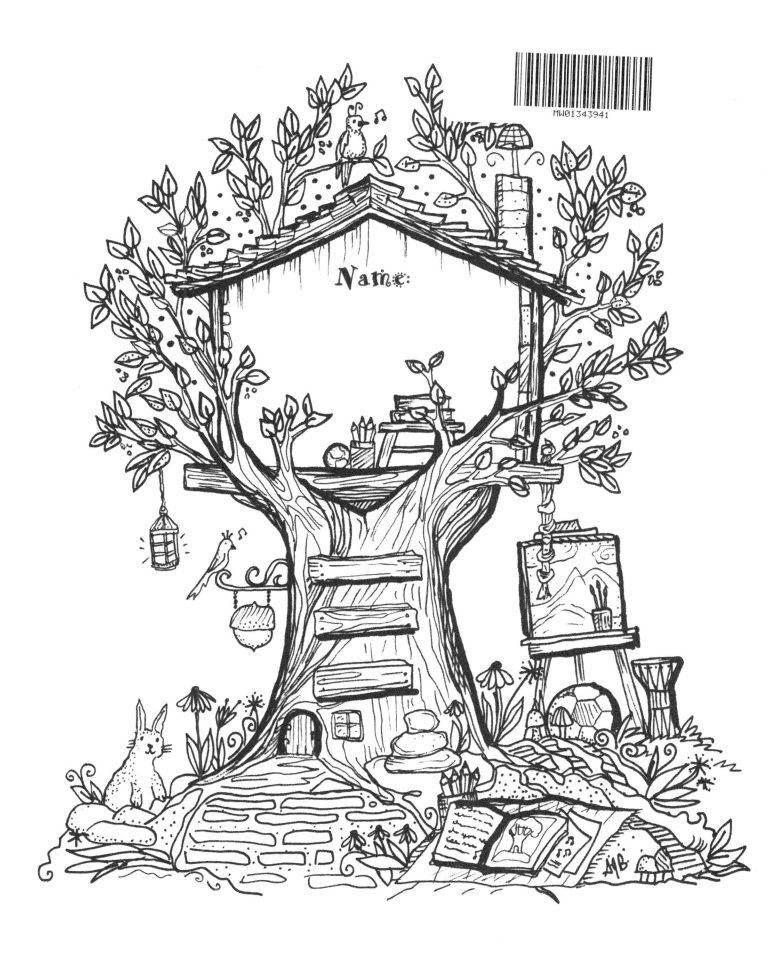

About the Writer's Fun-Schooling Journal

The Writer's Fun-Schooling Journal is for anybody who is interested in writing. This journal is designed to help writers develop and improve their skills. Students will work through a variety of writing challenge prompts designed to enhance their creativity, expand their vocabulary, and improve their written communication skills. To complete this guided learning journal, students need books, notebooks, and films/documentaries. Complete 5 pages per day for a 12-week plan or 10 pages per day for a 6-week plan.

Topics Covered Include:

Planning & setting priorities

Writing

Creative thinking

Reading

Film study

Oral practice

Vocabulary

Math practice

And more

The Thinking Tree

The Writer's Fun-Schooling Journal

Homeschooling Curriculum Handbook

For Students Majoring in Writing

Anna Miriam Brown

Sarah Janisse Brown

Copyright 2019

The Thinking Tree, LLC

FunSchooling.com

Instructions

Draw or list six things you want to learn about or writing skills you want to develop:

1.
2.
3.
4.
5.
6.

Action Steps:

1. Go to the library, your bookshelf, or a bookstore.
2. Choose a total of nine books about these topics or skills.
3. Gather your supplies and get creative!
4. Use 5 pages each day to develop your skills as a writer.

Supplies Needed:

You will need books, notebooks, pencils, pens and films/documentaries.

Choose your books

Pick out 9 different books that will help you study and develop writing skills

Draw the covers and titles here:

Plans & Priorities

Date: _____

To-do List:
_____
_____
_____
_____

A Quote:
_____
_____
_____
_____

My Goals:
_____
_____
_____
_____

Describe Today's Emotions:
_____
_____
_____
_____

Today I am grateful for:
_____
_____
_____
_____

Creative Writing

Use this page for a short story or diary entry.

Add an illustration.

Reading Time!

Choose a few books from your stack to focus on today.
Write down or draw anything that inspires you.
(Set a timer for 1 hour)

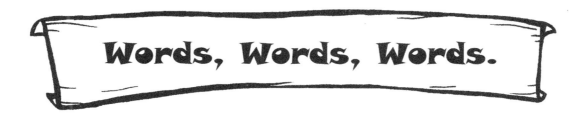
Words, Words, Words.

Write down ten words you liked from your reading time.
Using a thesaurus, look up related words and write them down too.

Thesaurus Words

_____   _____

_____   _____

_____   _____

_____   _____

_____   _____

_____   _____

_____   _____

_____   _____

_____   _____

_____   _____

WORD OF THE DAY:

What was your favorite word today and why?

_____

_____

_____

Screen Time

Watch a movie that was inspired by a book or true story.

Title:
_____

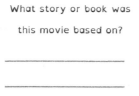

What story or book was this movie based on?
_____
_____
_____

Quotes

Write down your favorite quotes from the movie.

_____
_____
_____
_____
_____
_____
_____
_____

Rating:

Worst

Bad

Awful

Ok

Nice

Great

Best

Dialogue!

Be creative and practice writing dialogue.

Character Names:

Title_____

_____

_____

Writing Challenge

Write a Short Story

You wake up in a foreign land, not remembering how you got there or why you're there. Suddenly, a sharp pain goes through your left shoulder...

_____
_____
_____
_____
_____
_____
_____
_____
_____
_____
_____
_____
_____
_____
_____
_____
_____
_____
_____
_____
_____
_____
_____

If you need more writing space, use a notebook.

Listening Time

Listen to an Audio Book or Podcast.
Color the picture below while you tune in!

Title_____

Create a Comic

Create a comic based on a story you love or one you are writing!

TITLE:_____

Plans & Priorities

Date: _____

To-do List:
_____
_____
_____
_____

A Quote:
_____
_____
_____
_____

My Goals:
_____
_____
_____
_____

Describe Today's Emotions:
_____
_____
_____
_____

Yesterday's Best Memory:
_____
_____
_____
_____
_____

Copywork

Copy an excerpt from an inspiring speech.

Title: _____

Author/Source: _____ Year Written: _____

Reading Time!

Choose a few books from your stack to focus on today.

Write down or draw anything that inspires you.

(Set a timer for 1 hour)

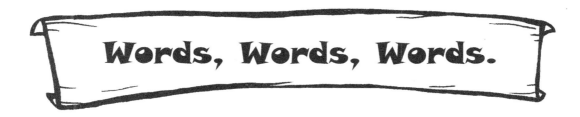

Words, Words, Words.

Write down ten words you liked from your reading time.
Using a thesaurus, look up related words and write them down too.

Thesaurus Words

_____   _____
_____   _____
_____   _____
_____   _____
_____   _____
_____   _____
_____   _____
_____   _____
_____   _____
_____   _____

WORD OF THE DAY:

What was your favorite word today and why?
_____
_____

Screen Time

Watch a movie that was inspired by a book or true story.

Title:

_____

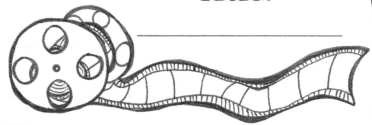

What story or book was this movie based on?

_____
_____
_____

Quotes

Write down your favorite quotes from the movie.

_____
_____
_____
_____
_____
_____
_____
_____
_____
_____

Rating:

Worst

Bad

Awful

Ok

Nice

Great

Best

Dialogue!

Be creative and practice writing dialogue.

Title_____

Character Names:

_____

_____

Writing Challenge

Word Make-Over

What words do you frequently use in your writings that could use a make-over? Come on. Everyone has them. Maybe they're words like said, happy, and nice. Make a list of your 20 most commonly used words, and then pull out a thesaurus. What new and exciting synonyms can you find to replace those boring, overused words? You'll be surprised how many new words will spark you. Out with the old and in with fresh, interesting words like remarked, ecstatic, and pleasant.

If you need more writing space, use a notebook.

Book of the Day

Choose a novel to focus on today. Choose a section to copy and after you're done, read it aloud seven times.

Title_____

Story Board

Create a story board based on a story you love or one you are writing!

TITLE:_____

Plans & Priorities

Date:_____

To-do List:
_____
_____
_____
_____

A Quote:
_____
_____
_____
_____

My Goals:
_____
_____
_____
_____

Describe Today's Emotions:
_____
_____
_____
_____

Today I am grateful for:
_____
_____
_____
_____

Creative Writing

Use this page for a short story or diary entry.

Add an illustration.

Reading Time!

Choose a few books from your stack to focus on today.

Write down or draw anything that inspires you.

(Set a timer for 1 hour)

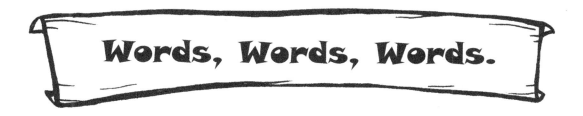
Words, Words, Words.

Write down ten words you liked from your reading time.
Using a thesaurus, look up related words and write them down too.

Thesaurus Words

_____   _____

_____   _____

_____   _____

_____   _____

_____   _____

_____   _____

_____   _____

_____   _____

_____   _____

_____   _____

WORD OF THE DAY:

What was your favorite word today and why?

_____

_____

_____

Screen Time

Watch a movie that was inspired by a book or true story.

Title:
_____

What story or book was this movie based on?
_____
_____
_____

Quotes

Write down your favorite quotes from the movie.

_____
_____
_____
_____
_____
_____
_____
_____
_____
_____

Rating:

Worst

Bad

Awful

Ok

Nice

Great

Best

Dialogue!

Be creative and practice writing dialogue.

Title_____

Character Names:
_____
_____

Writing Challenge

Different Writing Genres

One of the most important things you can do as a writer is to study and copy the best works. For me that was The Hunger Games series. I chose those books because they had four times the number of reviews of any other books on Amazon. That says something.

As I read and studies those books, I couldn't put them down. I was eager to discover what made them so captivating. What I realized is The Hunger Games series is not just a thriller—not in the slightest.

Suzanne Collins didn't just have one style or genre in mind when she wrote this trilogy. She expertly incorporated so many different genres, and on such a high level. That's why this series is so loved. Because there is something for everyone. There is drama, adventure, mystery, poetry, nail-biting suspense and so much more.

So, when you write, keep the readers on their toes. Give them what they want but never how they expect it. This is what is going to make people believe they just found the most interesting story in the world. This is what will make your writing addictive. This is what makes a bestseller.

Use this page to brainstorm different genre combinations. Comedy/horror? Poetry/mystery? Thriller/romance? What will your style be?

_____
_____
_____
_____
_____

If you need more writing space, use a notebook.

Listening Time

Listen to an Audio Book or Podcast.

Color the picture below while you tune in!

Title_____

Create a Comic

Create a comic based on a story you love or one you are writing!

TITLE:_____

Plans & Priorities

Date: _____

To-do List:
_____
_____
_____
_____
_____

A Quote:
_____
_____
_____
_____
_____

My Goals:
_____
_____
_____
_____
_____

Describe Today's Emotions:
_____
_____
_____
_____

Yesterday's Best Memory:
_____
_____
_____
_____

Copywork

Copy a poem that you really enjoy.

Title: _____

Author/Source: _____ Year Written: _____

Reading Time!

Choose a few books from your stack to focus on today.

Write down or draw anything that inspires you.

(Set a timer for 1 hour)

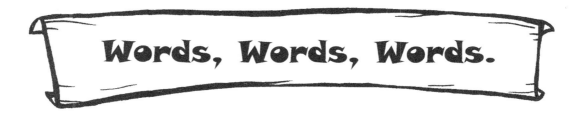
Words, Words, Words.

Write down ten words you liked from your reading time.
Using a thesaurus, look up related words and write them down too.

Thesaurus Words

_____   _____

_____   _____

_____   _____

_____   _____

_____   _____

_____   _____

_____   _____

_____   _____

_____   _____

_____   _____

WORD OF THE DAY:

What was your favorite word today and why?

_____

_____

Screen Time

Watch a movie that was inspired by a book or true story.

Title:
_____

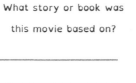

What story or book was this movie based on?
_____
_____
_____

Quotes

Write down your favorite quotes from the movie.

_____
_____
_____
_____
_____
_____
_____
_____

Rating:

Worst

Bad

Awful

Ok

Nice

Great

Best

Dialogue!

Be creative and practice writing dialogue.

Title _____

Character Names:
_____
_____

Writing Challenge

Write a "love at first sight" moment

Two people
Two pasts
One present
One chance

Think about these two characters. Design a past for each of them and then find a creative and romantic way to bring them together.

Write their first meeting. Where was it, why are they speaking, how do they feel? Make sure to bring their past into the way they talk and think. And write in some tension. Perfection is boring.

_____
_____
_____
_____
_____
_____
_____
_____
_____
_____
_____
_____
_____
_____
_____

If you need more writing space, use a notebook.

Book of the Day

Choose a novel to focus on today. Choose a section to copy and after you're done, read it aloud seven times.

Title_____

Story Board

Create a story board based on a story you love or one you are writing!

TITLE:_____

Plans & Priorities

Date:_____

To-do List:
_____
_____
_____
_____

A Quote:
_____
_____
_____
_____

My Goals:
_____
_____
_____
_____

Describe Today's Emotions:
_____
_____
_____
_____

Today I am grateful for-

_____
_____
_____
_____

Creative Writing

Use this page for a short story or diary entry.

Add an illustration.

_____
_____
_____
_____
_____
_____
_____
_____
_____
_____
_____
_____
_____
_____

Reading Time!

Choose a few books from your stack to focus on today.

Write down or draw anything that inspires you.

(Set a timer for 1 hour)

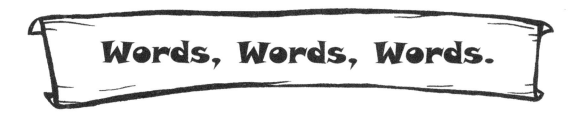

Words, Words, Words.

Write down ten words you liked from your reading time.
Using a thesaurus, look up related words and write them down too.

Thesaurus Words

_____   _____

_____   _____

_____   _____

_____   _____

_____   _____

_____   _____

_____   _____

_____   _____

_____   _____

_____   _____

WORD OF THE DAY:

What was your favorite word today and why?

_____

_____

Screen Time

Watch a movie that was inspired by a book or true story.

Title:
_____

What story or book was this movie based on?
_____
_____
_____

Quotes

Write down your favorite quotes from the movie.

_____
_____
_____
_____
_____
_____
_____
_____

Rating:

Worst

Bad

Awful

Ok

Nice

Great

Best

Dialogue!

Be creative and practice writing dialogue.

Title_____

Character Names:
_____
_____

Writing Challenge

Write a live dialogue

While hanging out with your friends and family, pull out a pen and start writing what you hear. This will help your mind understand the flow of real conversation. Challenge yourself to do this every week. Make sure to keep your ears open—always—because life is full of jewels. Even the smallest exchange can spark inspiration that will lead to the creation of a whole story. The first time I had the idea to do this, I was playing the card game "Exploding Kittens" with my sisters. When I told Naomi I was writing her dialogue, she was not as thrilled as I was.

"Anna, you are so annoying! No one likes you when you're like this!" Naomi says.

"What on Earth, Namie? Literally, what am I doing?" She give me a dirty look.

"You said you're gonna write my *dialogue*. Why the heck do you want to write my dialogue or strategy or whatever?"

I begin to laugh. "Namie," I say, "Do you even know what a dialogue is?"

A smile begins to mix with her determined, annoyed expression. "No!" she yells. Her anger breaks and we both start laughing.

"Namie, writing your dialogue just means that I write down what you're saying."

"But why the heck do you want to do that!?" she demands, still not convinced that I don't want to study her spectacular card-laying strategy.

"It's literally for me to practice writing," I explain.

She goes back to shuffling the deck and says, "What on Earth, Anna?"

If you need more writing space, use a notebook.

Listening Time

Listen to an Audio Book or Podcast.
Color the picture below while you tune in!

Title _____

Create a Comic

Create a comic based on a story you love or one you are writing!

TITLE:_____

Plans & Priorities

Date: _____

To-do List:
_____
_____
_____
_____

A Quote:
_____
_____
_____
_____

My Goals:
_____
_____
_____
_____

Describe Today's Emotions:
_____
_____
_____
_____

Yesterday's Best Memory:

_____
_____
_____
_____

Copywork

Copy an excerpt from an interesting play.

Title: _____

Author/Source: _____ Year Written: _____

Reading Time!

Choose a few books from your stack to focus on today.

Write down or draw anything that inspires you.

(Set a timer for 1 hour)

Words, Words, Words.

Write down ten words you liked from your reading time.
Using a thesaurus, look up related words and write them down too.

Thesaurus Words

_____   _____
_____   _____
_____   _____
_____   _____
_____   _____
_____   _____
_____   _____
_____   _____
_____   _____
_____   _____

WORD OF THE DAY:

What was your favorite word today and why?
_____
_____

Screen Time

Watch a movie that was inspired by a book or true story.

Title:
_____

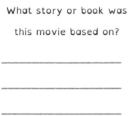

What story or book was this movie based on?
_____
_____
_____

Quotes

Write down your favorite quotes from the movie.

_____
_____
_____
_____
_____
_____
_____
_____

Rating:

Worst

Bad

Awful

Ok

Nice

Great

Best

Dialogue!

Be creative and practice writing dialogue.

Character Names:

Title _____   _____
                       _____

Writing Challenge

Location Description

Take this book somewhere you find beautiful and inspiring. Write what you see and how it makes you feel. Don't just look. *See*. Include smell, touch, taste and other senses as well. Include your soul.

If you need more writing space, use a notebook.

Book of the Day

Choose a novel to focus on today. Choose a section to copy and after you're done, read it aloud seven times.

Title_____

Story Board

Create a story board based on a story you love or one you are writing!

TITLE:_____

Plans & Priorities

Date:_____

To-do List:
_____
_____
_____
_____

A Quote:
_____
_____
_____
_____

My Goals:
_____
_____
_____
_____

Describe Today's Emotions:
_____
_____
_____
_____

Today I am grateful for:
_____
_____
_____
_____
_____

Creative Writing

Use this page for a short story or diary entry.

Add an illustration.

Reading Time!

Choose a few books from your stack to focus on today.

Write down or draw anything that inspires you.

(Set a timer for 1 hour)

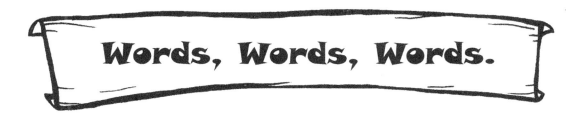

Words, Words, Words.

Write down ten words you liked from your reading time.
Using a thesaurus, look up related words and write them down too.

Thesaurus Words

_____   _____
_____   _____
_____   _____
_____   _____
_____   _____
_____   _____
_____   _____
_____   _____
_____   _____
_____   _____

WORD OF THE DAY:

What was your favorite word today and why?

_____
_____

Screen Time

Watch a movie that was inspired by a book or true story.

Title:

_____

What story or book was this movie based on?
_____
_____
_____

Quotes

Write down your favorite quotes from the movie.

_____
_____
_____
_____
_____
_____
_____
_____
_____
_____

Rating:

Worst

Bad

Awful

Ok

Nice

Great

Best

Dialogue!

Be creative and practice writing dialogue.

Title_____

Character Names:

_____

_____

Writing Challenge

The Song Game

- Put your playlist on shuffle.

- Design a character inspired by the first song that plays.

- Design another character inspired by the second song that plays.

- The third song that plays describes their relationship. (Doesn't have to be romantic)

- Now, write a short story.

_____
_____
_____
_____
_____
_____
_____
_____
_____
_____
_____
_____
_____
_____
_____
_____
_____

If you need more writing space, use a notebook.

Listening Time

Listen to an Audio Book or Podcast.
Color the picture below while you tune in!

Title_____

Create a Comic

Create a comic based on a story you love or one you are writing!

TITLE:_____

Plans & Priorities

Date: _____

To-do List:
_____
_____
_____
_____
_____

A Quote:
_____
_____
_____
_____
_____

My Goals:
_____
_____
_____
_____
_____

Describe Today's Emotions:
_____
_____
_____
_____
_____

Yesterday's Best Memory:
_____
_____
_____
_____
_____

Copywork

Copy an article from a newspaper or news blog.

Title: _____

Author/Source: _____ Year Written: _____

Reading Time!

Choose a few books from your stack to focus on today.

Write down or draw anything that inspires you.

(Set a timer for 1 hour)

Words, Words, Words.

Write down ten words you liked from your reading time.
Using a thesaurus, look up related words and write them down too.

Thesaurus Words

_____ _____

_____ _____

_____ _____

_____ _____

_____ _____

_____ _____

_____ _____

_____ _____

_____ _____

_____ _____

WORD OF THE DAY:

What was your favorite word today and why?

_____
_____

Screen Time

Watch a movie that was inspired by a book or true story.

Title:
_____

What story or book was this movie based on?
_____
_____
_____

Quotes

Write down your favorite quotes from the movie.

_____
_____
_____
_____
_____
_____
_____
_____
_____
_____

Rating:

Worst

Bad

Awful

Ok

Nice

Great

Best

Dialogue!

Be creative and practice writing dialogue.

Title_____

Character Names:
_____
_____

Writing Challenge

Balance

In a good story, the hero isn't perfect and the villain has admirable qualities. Keep this in mind, especially when writing villains. Their reason for being the way they are shouldn't simply be "pure evil." Maybe they have a painful past; maybe they were even good at one time. Showing that makes the character more vulnerable and endearing. Readers will connect more to realistic characters.

Let the heroes have their flaws and let the villains have their virtues. On this page design two characters: a hero and a villain. Write a couple paragraphs about each, giving backstory while revealing their present character. Show in the way they speak what past events may have affected them, positively or negatively.

Be creative and surprise yourself.

If you need more writing space, use a notebook.

Book of the Day

Choose a novel to focus on today. Choose a section to copy and after you're done, read it aloud seven times.

Title_____

Story Board

Create a story board based on a story you love or one you are writing!

TITLE:_____

Plans & Priorities

Date:_____

To-do List:
_____
_____
_____
_____
_____

A Quote:
_____
_____
_____
_____
_____

My Goals:
_____
_____
_____
_____

Describe Today's Emotions:
_____
_____
_____
_____
_____

Today I am grateful for:

_____
_____
_____
_____

Creative Writing

Use this page for a short story or diary entry.

Add an illustration.

Reading Time!

Choose a few books from your stack to focus on today.

Write down or draw anything that inspires you.

(Set a timer for 1 hour)

Words, Words, Words.

Write down ten words you liked from your reading time.
Using a thesaurus, look up related words and write them down too.

Thesaurus Words

_____   _____
_____   _____
_____   _____
_____   _____
_____   _____
_____   _____
_____   _____
_____   _____
_____   _____
_____   _____

WORD OF THE DAY:

What was your favorite word today and why?

_____
_____

Screen Time

Watch a movie that was inspired by a book or true story.

Title:

_____

What story or book was this movie based on?

_____
_____
_____

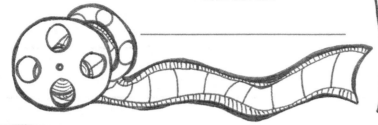

Quotes

Write down your favorite quotes from the movie.

_____
_____
_____
_____
_____
_____
_____
_____
_____
_____

Rating:

Worst

Bad

Awful

Ok

Nice

Great

Best

Dialogue!

Be creative and practice writing dialogue.

Title _____

Character Names:

_____

_____

Writing Challenge

Adventure Story Prompt

Someone discovers they have superpowers. Write their story. Make it heart-wrenching and triumphant.

_____
_____
_____
_____
_____
_____
_____
_____
_____
_____
_____
_____
_____
_____
_____
_____
_____
_____
_____
_____
_____
_____
_____
_____
_____

If you need more writing space, use a notebook.

Listening Time

Listen to an Audio Book or Podcast.

Color the picture below while you tune in!

Title_____

Create a Comic

Create a comic based on a story you love or one you are writing!

TITLE:_____

Plans & Priorities

Date: _____

To-do List:
_____
_____
_____
_____

A Quote:
_____
_____
_____
_____

My Goals:
_____
_____
_____
_____

Describe Today's Emotions:
_____
_____
_____
_____

Yesterday's Best Memory:
_____
_____
_____
_____

Copywork

Copy an excerpt from a screenplay.

Title: _____

Author/Source: _____ Year Written: _____

Reading Time!

Choose a few books from your stack to focus on today.

Write down or draw anything that inspires you.

(Set a timer for 1 hour)

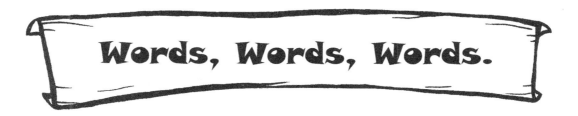

Words, Words, Words.

Write down ten words you liked from your reading time.
Using a thesaurus, look up related words and write them down too.

Thesaurus Words

_____   _____

_____   _____

_____   _____

_____   _____

_____   _____

_____   _____

_____   _____

_____   _____

_____   _____

_____   _____

WORD OF THE DAY:

What was your favorite word today and why?

_____
_____
_____

Screen Time

Watch a movie that was inspired by a book or true story.

Title:
_____

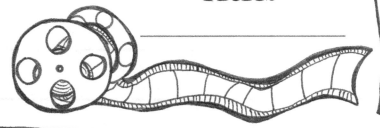

What story or book was this movie based on?
_____
_____
_____

Quotes

Write down your favorite quotes from the movie.

_____
_____
_____
_____
_____
_____
_____
_____
_____
_____

Rating:

Worst

Bad

Awful

Ok

Nice

Great

Best

Dialogue!

Be creative and practice writing dialogue.

Title_____

Character Names:
_____
_____

Writing Challenge

Thriller Story Prompt

You wake up in the dark. You can't remember where you are. You can't remember who you are.

_____
_____
_____
_____
_____
_____
_____
_____
_____
_____
_____
_____
_____
_____
_____
_____
_____
_____
_____
_____
_____
_____

If you need more writing space, use a notebook.

Book of the Day

Choose a novel to focus on today. Choose a section to copy and after you're done, read it aloud seven times.

Title _____

Story Board

Create a story board based on a story you love or one you are writing!

TITLE:_____

Plans & Priorities

Date:_____

To-do List:
_____
_____
_____
_____
_____

A Quote:
_____
_____
_____
_____

My Goals:
_____
_____
_____
_____
_____

Describe Today's Emotions:
_____
_____
_____
_____

Today I am grateful for:

Creative Writing

Use this page for a short story or diary entry.

Add an illustration.

Reading Time!

Choose a few books from your stack to focus on today.

Write down or draw anything that inspires you.

(Set a timer for 1 hour)

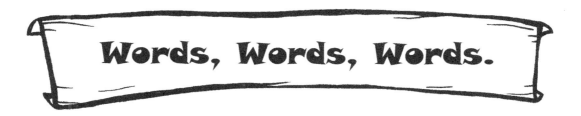
Words, Words, Words.

Write down ten words you liked from your reading time.
Using a thesaurus, look up related words and write them down too.

Thesaurus Words

WORD OF THE DAY:

What was your favorite word today and why?

Screen Time

Watch a movie that was inspired by a book or true story.

Title:

_____

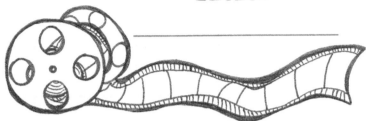

What story or book was this movie based on?

_____
_____
_____

Quotes

Write down your favorite quotes from the movie.

_____
_____
_____
_____
_____
_____
_____
_____
_____

Rating:

Worst

Bad

Awful

Ok

Nice

Great

Best

Dialogue!

Be creative and practice writing dialogue.

Title_____

Character Names:

_____

_____

Writing Challenge

READ!

If written words had volume, the way I write this would be deafening. You need to read. Read what people love. Read your favorites over and over and over because what you read will come out in your writing.

What you read will help you discover and settle on your own writing style. That's so important. When I first got into writing I did research on the world's most admired books, ordered them, and read them all. Doing this helps you discover what books people love, and your brain will subconsciously memorize patterns in the authors' writing styles. When you write, without even trying, you will use those same patterns. It's amazing how God made us. Don't read low quality books unless you keep a mental notepad of "how not to write."

Do your own research and make your own "Top Books List." For each book you read, copy your favorite part.

_____
_____
_____
_____
_____
_____
_____
_____
_____
_____
_____
_____
_____
_____
_____

If you need more writing space, use a notebook.

Listening Time

Listen to an Audio Book or Podcast.
Color the picture below while you tune in!

Title_____

Create a Comic

Create a comic based on a story you love or one you are writing!

TITLE:_____

Plans & Priorities

Date: _____

To-do List:
_____
_____
_____
_____

A Quote:
_____
_____
_____
_____

My Goals:
_____
_____
_____
_____

Describe Today's Emotions:
_____
_____
_____
_____

Yesterday's Best Memory:
_____
_____
_____
_____
_____

Copywork

Copy an excerpt from a popular children's book.

Title: _____

Author/Source: _____ Year Written: _____

Reading Time!

Choose a few books from your stack to focus on today.
Write down or draw anything that inspires you.
(Set a timer for 1 hour)

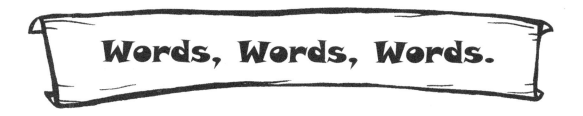

Words, Words, Words.

Write down ten words you liked from your reading time.
Using a thesaurus, look up related words and write them down too.

Thesaurus Words

_____   _____

_____   _____

_____   _____

_____   _____

_____   _____

_____   _____

_____   _____

_____   _____

_____   _____

_____   _____

WORD OF THE DAY:

What was your favorite word today and why?

_____

_____

Screen Time

Watch a movie that was inspired by a book or true story.

Title:

_____

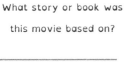

What story or book was this movie based on?

_____
_____
_____

Quotes

Write down your favorite quotes from the movie.

_____
_____
_____
_____
_____
_____
_____
_____

Rating:

Worst

Bad

Awful

Ok

Nice

Great

Best

Dialogue!

Be creative and practice writing dialogue.

Title_____

Character Names:
_____
_____

Writing Challenge

Drama Story Prompt

Twins who were separated at birth meet by chance. Try to write their story differently than the popular stories that are coming to your mind. Have fun with this! How would you feel if you met your long-lost twin? What if he or she was a terrible person?

If you need more writing space, use a notebook.

Book of the Day

Choose a novel to focus on today. Choose a section to copy and after you're done, read it aloud seven times.

Title_____

Story Board

Create a story board based on a story you love or one you are writing!

TITLE:_____

Plans & Priorities

Date:_____

To-do List:

A Quote:

My Goals:

Describe Today's Emotions:

Today I am grateful for:

Creative Writing

Use this page for a short story or diary entry.

Add an illustration.

Reading Time!

Choose a few books from your stack to focus on today.

Write down or draw anything that inspires you.

(Set a timer for 1 hour)

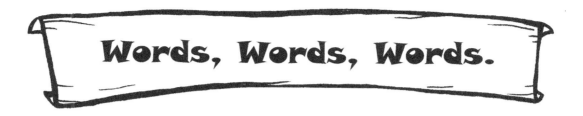
Words, Words, Words.

Write down ten words you liked from your reading time.
Using a thesaurus, look up related words and write them down too.

Thesaurus Words

_____   _____

_____   _____

_____   _____

_____   _____

_____   _____

_____   _____

_____   _____

_____   _____

_____   _____

_____   _____

WORD OF THE DAY:

What was your favorite word today and why?

_____
_____
_____

Screen Time

Watch a movie that was inspired by a book or true story.

Title:
_____

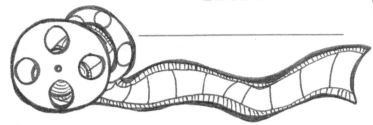

What story or book was this movie based on?
_____
_____
_____

Quotes

Write down your favorite quotes from the movie.

_____
_____
_____
_____
_____
_____
_____
_____
_____
_____

Rating:

Worst

Bad

Awful

Ok

Nice

Great

Best

Dialogue!

Be creative and practice writing dialogue.

Character Names:

Title_____

_____

_____

Writing Challenge

Three Cups and a Genius

Get three cups. Fill one cup with little papers that each have a different genre: drama, thriller, comedy, romance, adventure, etc. Fill another cup with themes: small town life, alien invasion, zombie apocalypse, pet store, lost in the wilderness, etc. Fill the third cup with characters: James, extroverted, fun, extreme germaphobe; Leah, shy, pretty, likes to be alone; Lucas, funny, handsome, bipolar, chef, etc.

After you've finished, pull one slip of paper from the "Genre" jar and the "Theme" jar and two from the "Character" jar. Then, write a story using those ideas. Do this a few times a week to exercise creativity or use it when you need an idea. Now, be a genius and write your story here.

_____
_____
_____
_____
_____
_____
_____
_____
_____
_____
_____
_____

If you need more writing space, use a notebook.

Listening Time

Listen to an Audio Book or Podcast.
Color the picture below while you tune in!

Title_____

Create a Comic

Create a comic based on a story you love or one you are writing!

TITLE:_____

Plans & Priorities

Date:_____

To-do List:
_____
_____
_____
_____
_____

A Quote:
_____
_____
_____
_____

My Goals:
_____
_____
_____
_____

Describe Today's Emotions:
_____
_____
_____
_____
_____

Yesterday's Best Memory:
_____
_____
_____
_____
_____

Copywork

Copy an excerpt from an advertisement.

Title: _____

Author/Source: _____ Year Written: _____

Reading Time!

Choose a few books from your stack to focus on today.

Write down or draw anything that inspires you.

(Set a timer for 1 hour)

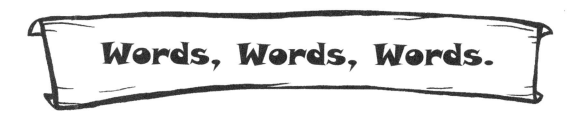

Words, Words, Words.

Write down ten words you liked from your reading time.
Using a thesaurus, look up related words and write them down too.

Thesaurus Words

_____   _____
_____   _____
_____   _____
_____   _____
_____   _____
_____   _____
_____   _____
_____   _____
_____   _____
_____   _____

WORD OF THE DAY:

What was your favorite word today and why?

_____
_____

Screen Time

Watch a movie that was inspired by a book or true story.

Title:
_____

What story or book was this movie based on?
_____
_____
_____

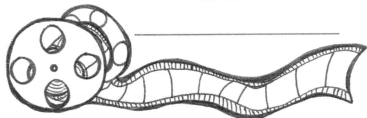

Quotes

Write down your favorite quotes from the movie.

_____
_____
_____
_____
_____
_____
_____
_____
_____
_____

Rating:

Worst

Bad

Awful

Ok

Nice

Great

Best

Dialogue!

Be creative and practice writing dialogue.

Character Names:

Title _____

_____

_____

Writing Challenge

Horror Dialogue Prompt

Something that shouldn't be talking starts talking to the house sitter.

If you need more writing space, use a notebook.

Book of the Day

Choose a novel to focus on today. Choose a section to copy and after you're done, read it aloud seven times.

Title_____

Story Board

Create a story board based on a story you love or one you are writing!

TITLE:_____

Plans & Priorities

Date: _____

To-do List:
_____
_____
_____
_____
_____

A Quote:
_____
_____
_____
_____
_____

My Goals:
_____
_____
_____
_____
_____

Describe Today's Emotions:
_____
_____
_____
_____
_____

Today I am grateful for:
_____
_____
_____
_____
_____

Creative Writing

Use this page for a short story or diary entry.

Add an illustration.

Reading Time!

Choose a few books from your stack to focus on today.

Write down or draw anything that inspires you.

(Set a timer for 1 hour)

Words, Words, Words.

Write down ten words you liked from your reading time.
Using a thesaurus, look up related words and write them down too.

Thesaurus Words

_____   _____
_____   _____
_____   _____
_____   _____
_____   _____
_____   _____
_____   _____
_____   _____
_____   _____
_____   _____

WORD OF THE DAY:

What was your favorite word today and why?

_____
_____
_____

Screen Time

Watch a movie that was inspired by a book or true story.

Title:

_____

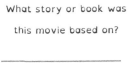

What story or book was this movie based on?

_____
_____
_____

Quotes

Write down your favorite quotes from the movie.

_____
_____
_____
_____
_____
_____
_____
_____

Rating:

Worst

Bad

Awful

Ok

Nice

Great

Best

Dialogue!

Be creative and practice writing dialogue.

Title_____

Character Names:
_____
_____

Writing Challenge

A Better Way

So many writers use the same cliché phrases all day long. But remember, just because it's what naturally flows from your pen doesn't mean it's good. As a writer, make it your goal to develop unique characters who have their own style and pattern of speech. If you have to say something that's often said, try to think of a fresh, new way of saying it.

Avoid clichés unless your character is specifically designed to talk that way. What are some lines and phrases you've seen a lot and want to avoid in your writing? Write them down and then write them in a more unique way.

Here are a few you can start with:
- Just the tip of the iceberg
- Avoid it like the plague
- But at the end of the day
- Think outside the box

Blah, blah, blah.

I understand almost everything has been done and every story told. But the thing is, 80% of what makes a great book isn't the story itself, it's how it is told. As you read, keep your eye open for clichés and when you find one, think about how you could write it in a better way.

_____
_____
_____
_____
_____

If you need more writing space, use a notebook.

Listening Time

Listen to an Audio Book or Podcast.
Color the picture below while you tune in!

Title_____

Create a Comic

Create a comic based on a story you love or one you are writing!

TITLE:_____

Plans & Priorities

Date: _____

To-do List:
_____
_____
_____
_____

A Quote:
_____
_____
_____
_____

My Goals:
_____
_____
_____
_____

Describe Today's Emotions:
_____
_____
_____
_____

Yesterday's Best Memory:

_____
_____
_____
_____
_____

Copywork

Copy an excerpt from a magazine article.

Title: _____

Author/Source: _____ Year Written: _____

Reading Time!

Choose a few books from your stack to focus on today.

Write down or draw anything that inspires you.

(Set a timer for 1 hour)

Words, Words, Words.

Write down ten words you liked from your reading time.
Using a thesaurus, look up related words and write them down too.

Thesaurus Words

WORD OF THE DAY:

What was your favorite word today and why?

Screen Time

Watch a movie that was inspired by a book or true story.

Title:

_____

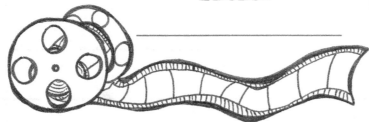

What story or book was this movie based on?

_____
_____
_____

Quotes

Write down your favorite quotes from the movie.

_____
_____
_____
_____
_____
_____
_____
_____

Rating:

Worst

Bad

Awful

Ok

Nice

Great

Best

Dialogue!

Be creative and practice writing dialogue.

Title_____

Character Names:

_____

_____

Writing Challenge

Movies and a Reason to Watch Them

When I first started writing, I made a list of all the best movies. I wanted to study interesting and realistic dialogue. Every week I cozied up on the couch with a pen and paper, watched one of the those movies, and wrote down the dialogue.

The first week I jotted down dialogue from "Pride and Prejudice." The chemistry was real in that one. Then, I copied dialogue from "Me Before You." Very romantic and made me laugh. Next, "Iron Man." Everyone loves that movie for a good reason. Stark's personality is what makes it.

I try to get my notebook every time I watch a movie and copy down the most golden moments. This will help bring your writing to the level of whatever you're watching.

Now, put in your favorite movie and start copying some dialogue!

_____
_____
_____
_____
_____
_____
_____
_____
_____
_____
_____
_____
_____

If you need more writing space, use a notebook.

Book of the Day

Choose a novel to focus on today. Choose a section to copy and after you're done, read it aloud seven times.

Title_____

Story Board

Create a story board based on a story you love or one you are writing!

TITLE:_____

Plans & Priorities

Date:_____

To-do List:
_____
_____
_____
_____
_____

A Quote:
_____
_____
_____
_____
_____

My Goals:
_____
_____
_____
_____
_____

Describe Today's Emotions:
_____
_____
_____
_____
_____

Today I am grateful for:
_____
_____
_____
_____

Creative Writing

Use this page for a short story or diary entry.

Add an illustration.

Reading Time!

Choose a few books from your stack to focus on today.

Write down or draw anything that inspires you.

(Set a timer for 1 hour)

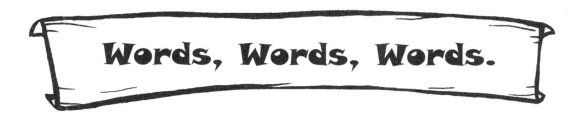

Words, Words, Words.

Write down ten words you liked from your reading time.
Using a thesaurus, look up related words and write them down too.

Thesaurus Words

_____   _____

_____   _____

_____   _____

_____   _____

_____   _____

_____   _____

_____   _____

_____   _____

_____   _____

_____   _____

WORD OF THE DAY:

What was your favorite word today and why?

_____

_____

Screen Time

Watch a movie that was inspired by a book or true story.

Title:
_____

What story or book was this movie based on?
_____
_____
_____

Quotes

Write down your favorite quotes from the movie.

_____
_____
_____
_____
_____
_____
_____
_____

Rating:

Worst

Bad

Awful

Ok

Nice

Great

Best

Dialogue!

Be creative and practice writing dialogue.

Title _____

Character Names:
_____
_____

Writing Challenge

Thriller Story Prompt

A plane crashes on the beach of a mysterious island. There are two and a half survivors....

If you need more writing space, use a notebook.

Listening Time

Listen to an Audio Book or Podcast.
Color the picture below while you tune in!

Title_____

Create a Comic

Create a comic based on a story you love or one you are writing!

TITLE:_____

Plans & Priorities

Date: _____

To-do List:
_____
_____
_____
_____

A Quote:
_____
_____
_____
_____

My Goals:
_____
_____
_____
_____

Describe Today's Emotions:
_____
_____
_____
_____

Yesterday's Best Memory:

_____
_____
_____
_____

Copywork

Copy the lyrics of an old song.

Title: _____

Author/Source: _____ Year Written: _____

_____
_____
_____
_____
_____
_____
_____
_____
_____
_____
_____
_____
_____
_____
_____
_____
_____
_____
_____
_____
_____
_____
_____
_____

Reading Time!

Choose a few books from your stack to focus on today.

Write down or draw anything that inspires you.

(Set a timer for 1 hour)

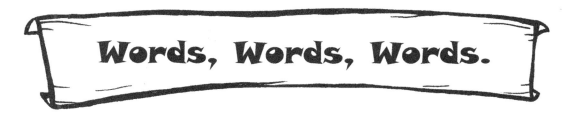
Words, Words, Words.

Write down ten words you liked from your reading time.
Using a thesaurus, look up related words and write them down too.

Thesaurus Words

_____   _____

_____   _____

_____   _____

_____   _____

_____   _____

_____   _____

_____   _____

_____   _____

_____   _____

_____   _____

WORD OF THE DAY:

What was your favorite word today and why?

_____
_____

Screen Time

Watch a movie that was inspired by a book or true story.

Title:
_____

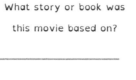

What story or book was this movie based on?
_____
_____
_____

Quotes

Write down your favorite quotes from the movie.

_____
_____
_____
_____
_____
_____
_____
_____

Rating:

Worst

Bad

Awful

Ok

Nice

Great

Best

Dialogue!

Be creative and practice writing dialogue.

Title_____

Character Names:
_____
_____

Writing Challenge

Copywork Works!

This may be the most important tip in this whole book. Copywork is what will subconsciously bring your writing to the same level as whatever you are copying. I'm not kidding. It will TRANSFORM your work.

No one really wants to just sit down and copy so what I do is meld my copy time and reading time together. I have a notebook called "Best Words Book" and I always read with it open and a pen in my hand. Whenever something strikes my heart and makes me feel something, good, bad, beautiful, etc., I write it down.

Again, this teaches your subconscious to write at the level of what you are reading. When you copy a sentence from a book, your brain thinks it is your own words and writing style. You don't need college to become a master. You just need a pen, paper, and patience.

When you read this week, write down parts of the story that inspire you and words that you find interesting.

_____
_____
_____
_____
_____
_____
_____
_____
_____
_____
_____
_____
_____

If you need more writing space, use a notebook.

Book of the Day

Choose a novel to focus on today. Choose a section to copy and after you're done, read it aloud seven times.

Title _____

Story Board

Create a story board based on a story you love or one you are writing!

TITLE:_____

Plans & Priorities

Date:_____

To-do List:
_____
_____
_____
_____

A Quote:
_____
_____
_____
_____

My Goals:
_____
_____
_____
_____

Describe Today's Emotions:
_____
_____
_____
_____

Today I am grateful for:
_____
_____
_____
_____

Creative Writing

Use this page for a short story or diary entry.

Add an illustration.

_____
_____
_____
_____
_____
_____
_____
_____
_____
_____
_____
_____
_____
_____
_____

Reading Time!

Choose a few books from your stack to focus on today.

Write down or draw anything that inspires you.

(Set a timer for 1 hour)

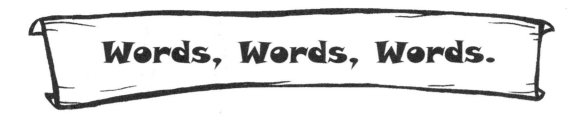
Words, Words, Words.

Write down ten words you liked from your reading time.
Using a thesaurus, look up related words and write them down too.

Thesaurus Words

WORD OF THE DAY:

What was your favorite word today and why?

Screen Time

Watch a movie that was inspired by a book or true story.

Title:

_____

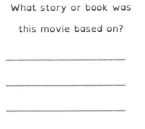

What story or book was this movie based on?

_____
_____
_____

Quotes

Write down your favorite quotes from the movie.

_____
_____
_____
_____
_____
_____
_____
_____
_____

Rating:

Worst

Bad

Awful

Ok

Nice

Great

Best

Dialogue!

Be creative and practice writing dialogue.

Title _____

Character Names:
_____
_____

Writing Challenge

Drama Story Prompt

Write a short story about a broken heart healing. Try to capture the emotions, to make yourself feel what your character is feeling.

The following example is a novelization of a story in Acts where Peter, Jesus' disciple, finally realizes that Jesus is with him, in a new way, and Peter is not alone. He experiences the triumphant freedom from fear and loneliness and the filling of the Spirit of God.

As tears began to blur my vision, my soul cries out with thanks. I can finally see! The Fire that appeared above my head makes its way to my heart, making its home in me. I grip my tunic and weep, rocking back and forth as tears of joy streak down my face. "Thank you that you're here, my Lord," I say over and over. Thank you that you never left."

Simple, but full of feeling. That's what you're going for.

If you need more writing space, use a notebook.

Listening Time

Listen to an Audio Book or Podcast.
Color the picture below while you tune in!

Title_____

Create a Comic

Create a comic based on a story you love or one you are writing!

TITLE:_____

Plans & Priorities

Date: _____

To-do List:
_____
_____
_____
_____
_____

A Quote:
_____
_____
_____
_____
_____

My Goals:
_____
_____
_____
_____
_____

Describe Today's Emotions:
_____
_____
_____
_____
_____

Yesterday's Best Memory:
_____
_____
_____
_____
_____

Copywork

Copy an excerpt from an instruction manual.

Title: _____

Author/Source: _____ Year Written: _____

Reading Time!

Choose a few books from your stack to focus on today.

Write down or draw anything that inspires you.

(Set a timer for 1 hour)

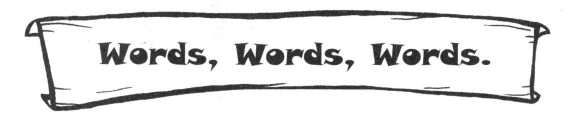
Words, Words, Words.

Write down ten words you liked from your reading time.
Using a thesaurus, look up related words and write them down too.

Thesaurus Words

_____   _____
_____   _____
_____   _____
_____   _____
_____   _____
_____   _____
_____   _____
_____   _____
_____   _____
_____   _____

WORD OF THE DAY:

What was your favorite word today and why?
_____
_____

Screen Time

Watch a movie that was inspired by a book or true story.

Title:
_____

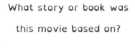

What story or book was this movie based on?
_____
_____
_____

Quotes

Write down your favorite quotes from the movie.

_____
_____
_____
_____
_____
_____
_____
_____
_____
_____

Rating:

Worst

Bad

Awful

Ok

Nice

Great

Best

Dialogue!

Be creative and practice writing dialogue.

Title _____

Character Names:
_____
_____

Writing Challenge

Keep Secrets

Put clues in the beginning of the novel, then draw your readers away. Build the suspense. At the end, clearly and thoroughly satisfy them with the big revelation.

Study the way other bestselling authors have done this. Readers love to feel like they are in on a secret. Maybe it's a secret one character knows and another does not. Keep your readers on the edge of their seats as you dramatically answer questions as characters get to know each other. Keep a balance between sharing a secret with your readers and keeping crucial information from them until the end.

Readers want drama, suspense. No one needs a boring book.

Practice writing a short story that is full of drama and suspense.

If you need more writing space, use a notebook.

Book of the Day

Choose a novel to focus on today. Choose a section to copy and after you're done, read it aloud seven times.

Title _____

Story Board

Create a story board based on a story you love or one you are writing!

TITLE:_____

Plans & Priorities

Date:_____

To-do List:
_____
_____
_____
_____

A Quote:
_____
_____
_____
_____

My Goals:
_____
_____
_____
_____

Describe Today's Emotions:
_____
_____
_____
_____

Today I am grateful for:
_____
_____
_____
_____

Creative Writing

Use this page for a short story or diary entry.

Add an illustration.

Reading Time!

Choose a few books from your stack to focus on today.

Write down or draw anything that inspires you.

(Set a timer for 1 hour)

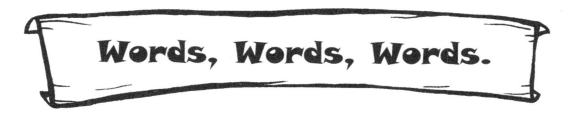

Words, Words, Words.

Write down ten words you liked from your reading time.
Using a thesaurus, look up related words and write them down too.

Thesaurus Words

_____   _____

_____   _____

_____   _____

_____   _____

_____   _____

_____   _____

_____   _____

_____   _____

_____   _____

_____   _____

WORD OF THE DAY:

What was your favorite word today and why?

_____
_____

Screen Time

Watch a movie that was inspired by a book or true story.

Title:
_____

What story or book was this movie based on?
_____
_____
_____

Quotes

Write down your favorite quotes from the movie.

_____
_____
_____
_____
_____
_____
_____
_____
_____

Rating:

Worst

Bad

Awful

Ok

Nice

Great

Best

Dialogue!

Be creative and practice writing dialogue.

Title_____

Character Names:
_____
_____

Writing Challenge

Comedy Dialogue Prompt

A couple meets at a fancy restaurant. One plans to propose; the other plans to break up.

If you need more writing space, use a notebook.

Listening Time

Listen to an Audio Book or Podcast.
Color the picture below while you tune in!

Title _____

Create a Comic

Create a comic based on a story you love or one you are writing!

TITLE:_____

Plans & Priorities

Date:_____

To-do List:
_____
_____
_____
_____
_____

A Quote:
_____
_____
_____
_____
_____

My Goals:
_____
_____
_____
_____

Describe Today's Emotions:
_____
_____
_____
_____

Yesterday's Best Memory:
_____
_____
_____
_____
_____

Copywork

Copy an excerpt from an old letter or diary.

Title: _____

Author/Source: _____ Year Written: _____

Reading Time!

Choose a few books from your stack to focus on today.

Write down or draw anything that inspires you.

(Set a timer for 1 hour)

Words, Words, Words.

Write down ten words you liked from your reading time.
Using a thesaurus, look up related words and write them down too.

Thesaurus Words

_____   _____
_____   _____
_____   _____
_____   _____
_____   _____
_____   _____
_____   _____
_____   _____
_____   _____
_____   _____

WORD OF THE DAY:

What was your favorite word today and why?

_____
_____

Screen Time

Watch a movie that was inspired by a book or true story.

Title:

_____

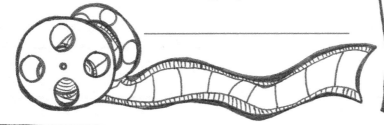

What story or book was this movie based on?

_____
_____
_____

Quotes

Write down your favorite quotes from the movie.

_____
_____
_____
_____
_____
_____
_____
_____

Rating:

Worst

Bad

Awful

Ok

Nice

Great

Best

Dialogue!

Be creative and practice writing dialogue.

Character Names:

Title _____   _____
                      _____

Writing Challenge

Kill the Filler

No book needs useless filler—not filler dialogue, monologues, or descriptions. Leave out the stuff you as a reader find repetitive and wordy. If you're not sure what to write, don't belabor the point. Instead, take a break, get a snack, brainstorm new ideas, and then come back to your writing and try again. Make something dramatic happen. You are the writer. The story is yours.

Practice writing a part of a story in 2 different ways: one that is quick, interesting, and to the point and the other with lots of unnecessary words and descriptions. Which sounds better to you? Which would sound better to your readers? This exercise will help your subconscious mind understand the difference between clear and concise writing vs. wordy writing.

If you need more writing space, use a notebook.

Book of the Day

Choose a novel to focus on today. Choose a section to copy and after you're done, read it aloud seven times.

Title_____

Story Board

Create a story board based on a story you love or one you are writing!

TITLE:_____

Plans & Priorities

Date: _____

To-do List:
_____
_____
_____
_____
_____

A Quote:
_____
_____
_____
_____
_____

My Goals:
_____
_____
_____
_____
_____

Describe Today's Emotions:
_____
_____
_____
_____

Today I am grateful for:

_____
_____
_____
_____
_____

Creative Writing

Use this page for a short story or diary entry.

Add an illustration.

Reading Time!

Choose a few books from your stack to focus on today.

Write down or draw anything that inspires you.

(Set a timer for 1 hour)

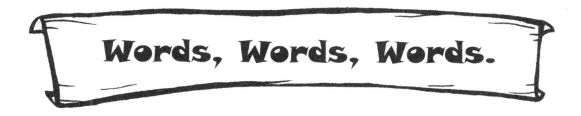

Words, Words, Words.

Write down ten words you liked from your reading time.
Using a thesaurus, look up related words and write them down too.

Thesaurus Words

_____   _____
_____   _____
_____   _____
_____   _____
_____   _____
_____   _____
_____   _____
_____   _____
_____   _____
_____   _____

WORD OF THE DAY:

What was your favorite word today and why?
_____
_____

Screen Time

Watch a movie that was inspired by a book or true story.

Title:
_____

What story or book was this movie based on?
_____
_____
_____

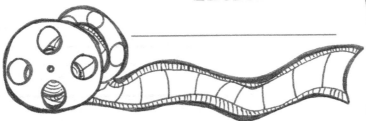

Quotes

Write down your favorite quotes from the movie.

_____
_____
_____
_____
_____
_____
_____
_____
_____
_____

Rating:

Worst

Bad

Awful

Ok

Nice

Great

Best

Dialogue!

Be creative and practice writing dialogue.

Title _____

Character Names:
_____
_____

Writing Challenge

The Power of Seven

Did you know that if you repeat something 7 times it will stick in your mind for the rest of your life? It's crazy.

Today, I want you to look through different sources to find writings that spark deep emotion like sadness, love, torment, fear, joy, humor, anger, etc. Look for these selections in your favorite books (fictions and non-fiction), blogs, essays, advertisements, plays, movie scripts, etc.

Use the space below and on the next page to copy your favorites. Spill into a notebook if you need more room! After you have finished, read each selection out loud 7 times each. Try saying them without looking at the page. This will burn the quality and style of writing into your mind better than anything else.

_____
_____
_____
_____
_____
_____
_____
_____
_____
_____
_____
_____
_____
_____

If you need more writing space, use a notebook.

Listening Time

Listen to an Audio Book or Podcast.
Color the picture below while you tune in!

Title_____

Create a Comic

Create a comic based on a story you love or one you are writing!

TITLE:_____

Plans & Priorities

Date: _____

To-do List:
_____
_____
_____
_____

A Quote:
_____
_____
_____
_____

My Goals:
_____
_____
_____
_____

Describe Today's Emotions:
_____
_____
_____
_____

Yesterday's Best Memory:
_____
_____
_____
_____
_____

Copywork

Copy an excerpt from an adventure story.

Title: _____

Author/Source: _____ Year Written: _____

Reading Time!

Choose a few books from your stack to focus on today.

Write down or draw anything that inspires you.

(Set a timer for 1 hour)

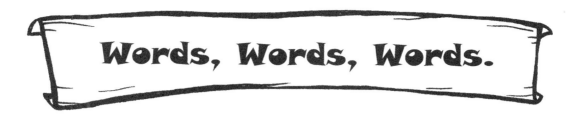

Words, Words, Words.

Write down ten words you liked from your reading time.
Using a thesaurus, look up related words and write them down too.

Thesaurus Words

_____   _____
_____   _____
_____   _____
_____   _____
_____   _____
_____   _____
_____   _____
_____   _____
_____   _____
_____   _____

WORD OF THE DAY:

What was your favorite word today and why?

_____
_____

Screen Time

Watch a movie that was inspired by a book or true story.

Title:
_____

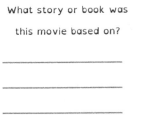

What story or book was this movie based on?
_____
_____
_____

Quotes

Write down your favorite quotes from the movie.

_____
_____
_____
_____
_____
_____
_____
_____
_____

Rating:

Worst

Bad

Awful

Ok

Nice

Great

Best

Dialogue!

Be creative and practice writing dialogue.

Character Names:

Title_____   _____
                      _____

Writing Challenge

Point of View Translation

Fiction novels are usually written in one of two points of view: first person or third person. Sometimes an author chooses to write in second person, but that is very rare.

My favorite point of view is first person. I love this POV because the character is telling the story. You get to see inside the character's head and watch the story unfold through that character's eyes. Consider this example from Angie Thomas' contemporary novel, The Hate You Give: "I can't change where I come from or what I've been through, so why should I be ashamed of what makes me, me?"

Other people prefer to write in third person. In third person POV, the author writes *about* the characters using pronouns like "he", "she", or "they." One great example of third person POV is found in Lois Lowry's dystopian novel, The Giver: "He heard people singing. Behind him, across vast distances of space and time, from the place he had left, he thought he heard music too. But perhaps it was only an echo."

Second person POV, characterized by use of the pronoun "you", is rarely used in fiction novels. However, there are some that use it well. Take for example the popular children's book, If You Give A Mouse a Cookie: "If you give a mouse a cookie, he's going to ask for a glass of milk. When you give him the milk, he'll probably ask you for a straw."

One of my favorite POV writing exercises is to sit down with a notebook and a book and find sections that make me feel deeply. I copy these sections into my notebook, changing the POV. For example, if the story is written in first person, I will rewrite it in third person. While I'm at it, I see if I can improve the original writing.

Grab a notebook and your favorite novel and try this exercise.

If you need more writing space, use a notebook.

Book of the Day

Choose a novel to focus on today. Choose a section to copy and after you're done, read it aloud seven times.

Title_____

Story Board

Create a story board based on a story you love or one you are writing!

TITLE:_____

Plans & Priorities

Date:_____

To-do List:
_____
_____
_____
_____

A Quote:
_____
_____
_____
_____

My Goals:
_____
_____
_____
_____

Describe Today's Emotions:
_____
_____
_____
_____

Today I am grateful for:
_____
_____
_____
_____

Creative Writing

Use this page for a short story or diary entry.

Add an illustration.

Reading Time!

Choose a few books from your stack to focus on today.

Write down or draw anything that inspires you.

(Set a timer for 1 hour)

Words, Words, Words.

Write down ten words you liked from your reading time.
Using a thesaurus, look up related words and write them down too.

Thesaurus Words

_____   _____

_____   _____

_____   _____

_____   _____

_____   _____

_____   _____

_____   _____

_____   _____

_____   _____

_____   _____

WORD OF THE DAY:

What was your favorite word today and why?

_____
_____

Screen Time

Watch a movie that was inspired by a book or true story.

Title:

_____

What story or book was this movie based on?

_____
_____
_____

Quotes

Write down your favorite quotes from the movie.

_____
_____
_____
_____
_____
_____
_____
_____
_____
_____

Rating:

Worst

Bad

Awful

Ok

Nice

Great

Best

Dialogue!

Be creative and practice writing dialogue.

Character Names:

Title _____   _____

_____

Writing Challenge

"Opening Up" Dialogue Prompt

Two people have a barrier breaking conversation where they both admit secret fears and struggles.

If you need more writing space, use a notebook.

Listening Time

Listen to an Audio Book or Podcast.
Color the picture below while you tune in!

Title _____

Create a Comic

Create a comic based on a story you love or one you are writing!

TITLE:_____

Plans & Priorities

Date:_____

To-do List:
_____
_____
_____
_____

A Quote:
_____
_____
_____
_____

My Goals:
_____
_____
_____
_____

Describe Today's Emotions:
_____
_____
_____
_____

Yesterday's Best Memory:

Copywork

Copy the first page of a classic novel.

Title: _____

Author/Source: _____ Year Written: _____

_____
_____
_____
_____
_____
_____
_____
_____
_____
_____
_____
_____
_____
_____
_____
_____
_____
_____
_____
_____
_____
_____
_____
_____
_____

Reading Time!

Choose a few books from your stack to focus on today.

Write down or draw anything that inspires you.

(Set a timer for 1 hour)

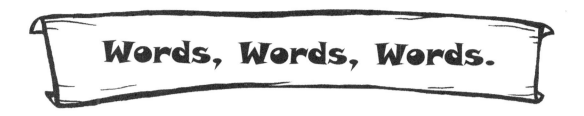

Words, Words, Words.

Write down ten words you liked from your reading time.
Using a thesaurus, look up related words and write them down too.

Thesaurus Words

_____   _____

_____   _____

_____   _____

_____   _____

_____   _____

_____   _____

_____   _____

_____   _____

_____   _____

_____   _____

WORD OF THE DAY:

What was your favorite word today and why?

_____
_____
_____

Screen Time

Watch a movie that was inspired by a book or true story.

Title:
_____

What story or book was this movie based on?
_____
_____
_____

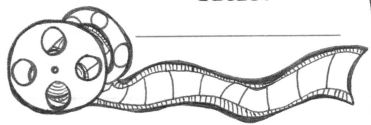

Quotes

Write down your favorite quotes from the movie.

_____
_____
_____
_____
_____
_____
_____
_____

Rating:

Worst

Bad

Awful

Ok

Nice

Great

Best

Dialogue!

Be creative and practice writing dialogue.

Title_____

Character Names:
_____
_____

Writing Challenge

Restaurant Writing

Next time you go to a restaurant, take this book. Write the dialogue for what you imagine is happening at a nearby table. Often, restaurant conversations are very interesting.

If you need more writing space, use a notebook.

Book of the Day

Choose a novel to focus on today. Choose a section to copy and after you're done, read it aloud seven times.

Title_____

Story Board

Create a story board based on a story you love or one you are writing!

TITLE:_____

Plans & Priorities

Date:_____

To-do List:
_____
_____
_____
_____
_____

A Quote:
_____
_____
_____
_____
_____

My Goals:
_____
_____
_____

Describe Today's Emotions:
_____
_____
_____
_____
_____

Today I am grateful for:
_____
_____
_____
_____
_____

Creative Writing

Use this page for a short story or diary entry.

Add an illustration.

_____
_____
_____
_____
_____
_____
_____
_____
_____
_____
_____
_____
_____
_____
_____

Reading Time!

Choose a few books from your stack to focus on today.

Write down or draw anything that inspires you.

(Set a timer for 1 hour)

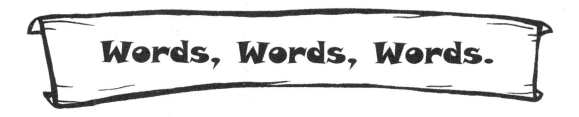

Words, Words, Words.

Write down ten words you liked from your reading time.
Using a thesaurus, look up related words and write them down too.

Thesaurus Words

_____   _____

_____   _____

_____   _____

_____   _____

_____   _____

_____   _____

_____   _____

_____   _____

_____   _____

_____   _____

WORD OF THE DAY:

What was your favorite word today and why?

_____
_____
_____

Screen Time

Watch a movie that was inspired by a book or true story.

Title:
_____

What story or book was this movie based on?
_____
_____
_____

Quotes

Write down your favorite quotes from the movie.

_____
_____
_____
_____
_____
_____
_____
_____
_____

Rating:

Worst

Bad

Awful

Ok

Nice

Great

Best

Dialogue!

Be creative and practice writing dialogue.

Title _____

Character Names:

_____

_____

Writing Challenge

Young Adult Comedy Dialogue Prompt

Write an awkward teenage love confession. Make it funny. and embarrassing.

If you need more writing space, use a notebook.

Listening Time

Listen to an Audio Book or Podcast.

Color the picture below while you tune in!

Title_____

Create a Comic

Create a comic based on a story you love or one you are writing!

TITLE:_____

Plans & Priorities

Date: _____

To-do List:
_____
_____
_____
_____
_____

A Quote:
_____
_____
_____
_____
_____

My Goals:
_____
_____
_____
_____
_____

Describe Today's Emotions:
_____
_____
_____
_____
_____

Yesterday's Best Memory:

_____
_____
_____
_____

Copywork

Copy the last page from your favorite novel.

Title: _____

Author/Source: _____ Year Written: _____

_____
_____
_____
_____
_____
_____
_____
_____
_____
_____
_____
_____
_____
_____
_____
_____
_____
_____
_____
_____
_____
_____
_____
_____

Reading Time!

Choose a few books from your stack to focus on today.

Write down or draw anything that inspires you.

(Set a timer for 1 hour)

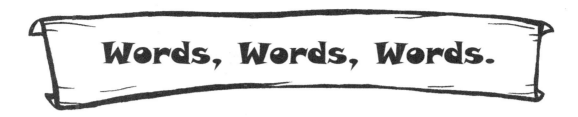
Words, Words, Words.

Write down ten words you liked from your reading time.
Using a thesaurus, look up related words and write them down too.

Thesaurus Words

_____   _____
_____   _____
_____   _____
_____   _____
_____   _____
_____   _____
_____   _____
_____   _____
_____   _____
_____   _____

WORD OF THE DAY:

What was your favorite word today and why?

_____
_____

Screen Time

Watch a movie that was inspired by a book or true story.

Title:
_____

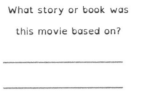

What story or book was this movie based on?
_____
_____
_____

Quotes

Write down your favorite quotes from the movie.

_____
_____
_____
_____
_____
_____
_____
_____
_____

Rating:

Worst

Bad

Awful

Ok

Nice

Great

Best

Dialogue!

Be creative and practice writing dialogue.

Title_____

Character Names:
_____
_____

Writing Challenge

Surprise Yourself

Write a couple lines of dialogue using two characters. Try not to overthink; just write what first comes to your mind.

Now, write it again. Start the same way, but make the second characters response be totally opposite of what you would expect. Let the conversation go a different way.

Rewrite this dialogue several more times, changing the way the second character responds each time. Which dialogue flows best? Which has the most surprises? Which makes the characters seem most captivating?

Consider the following example:

Character 1: Don't break my heart. Don't you dare break my heart!

Character 2 possible responses:
- I would never.
- Who do you think I am?
- I only will if you break mine.
- I guarantee I will.
- I can't make any promises.
- You know I'm no good at promises.
- I don't think I could if I tried.
- Don't tempt me.

Choose your favorite from the dialogues you wrote and continue writing the story.

If you need more writing space, use a notebook.

Book of the Day

Choose a novel to focus on today. Choose a section to copy and after you're done, read it aloud seven times.

Title_____

_____
_____
_____
_____
_____
_____
_____
_____
_____
_____
_____
_____
_____
_____
_____
_____
_____
_____

Story Board

Create a story board based on a story you love or one you are writing!

TITLE:_____

Plans & Priorities

Date:_____

To-do List:
_____
_____
_____
_____
_____

A Quote:
_____
_____
_____
_____
_____

My Goals:
_____
_____
_____
_____
_____

Describe Today's Emotions:
_____
_____
_____
_____
_____

Today I am grateful for:
_____
_____
_____
_____

Creative Writing

Use this page for a short story or diary entry.

Add an illustration.

Reading Time!

Choose a few books from your stack to focus on today.

Write down or draw anything that inspires you.

(Set a timer for 1 hour)

Words, Words, Words.

Write down ten words you liked from your reading time.
Using a thesaurus, look up related words and write them down too.

Thesaurus Words

WORD OF THE DAY:

What was your favorite word today and why?

Screen Time

Watch a movie that was inspired by a book or true story.

Title:

_____

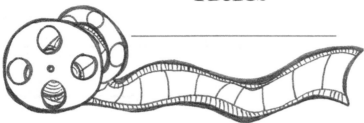

What story or book was this movie based on?

_____
_____
_____

Quotes

Write down your favorite quotes from the movie.

_____
_____
_____
_____
_____
_____
_____
_____
_____
_____

Rating:

Worst

Bad

Awful

Ok

Nice

Great

Best

Dialogue!

Be creative and practice writing dialogue.

Character Names:

Title _____

_____

_____

Writing Challenge

On Romance

First, we need to establish something: No one likes an "insta-romance." No kissing in Chapter 2. No saying "I love you," in Chapter 3.

If you're writing a romance, the whole point is the chemistry and suspense. Are the characters going to end up together? How is it going to happen? Draw this out as long as you can. Build the tension, feelings, and suspense for at least the first three quarters of the book. Let the love be real. Dreamy, but real.

If you need more writing space, use a notebook.

Listening Time

Listen to an Audio Book or Podcast.
Color the picture below while you tune in!

Title _____

Create a Comic

Create a comic based on a story you love or one you are writing!

TITLE:_____

Plans & Priorities

Date:_____

To-do List:
_____
_____
_____
_____

A Quote:
_____
_____
_____
_____

My Goals:
_____
_____
_____
_____

Describe Today's Emotions:
_____
_____
_____
_____

Yesterday's Best Memory:
_____
_____
_____
_____

Copywork

Copy an excerpt from a children's chapter book.

Title: _____

Author/Source: _____ Year Written: _____

Reading Time!

Choose a few books from your stack to focus on today.

Write down or draw anything that inspires you.

(Set a timer for 1 hour)

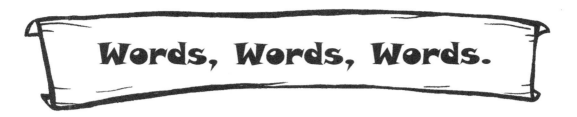

Words, Words, Words.

Write down ten words you liked from your reading time.
Using a thesaurus, look up related words and write them down too.

Thesaurus Words

_____   _____
_____   _____
_____   _____
_____   _____
_____   _____
_____   _____
_____   _____
_____   _____
_____   _____
_____   _____

WORD OF THE DAY:

What was your favorite word today and why?

_____
_____
_____

Screen Time

Watch a movie that was inspired by a book or true story.

Title:
_____

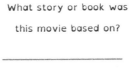

What story or book was this movie based on?
_____
_____
_____

Quotes

Write down your favorite quotes from the movie.

_____
_____
_____
_____
_____
_____
_____
_____
_____

Rating:

Worst

Bad

Awful

Ok

Nice

Great

Best

Dialogue!

Be creative and practice writing dialogue.

Title_____

Character Names:
_____
_____

Writing Challenge

Your Life Story Prompt

Use the space provided to write your life story. It can be any style or genre that you prefer: a realistic autobiography, fantasy, comedy, adventure, etc. Have fun with it and be creative.

If you need more writing space, use a notebook.

Book of the Day

Choose a novel to focus on today. Choose a section to copy and after you're done, read it aloud seven times.

Title_____

Story Board

Create a story board based on a story you love or one you are writing!

TITLE:_____

Fun-Schooling With Thinking Tree Books

Copyright Information

Thinking Tree Fun-Schooling Books and electronic printable downloads are for home and family use only. You may make copies of these materials for only the children in your household.

All other uses of this material must be with permission, in writing, by the Thinking Tree LLC. It is a violation of copyright law to distribute the electronic files or make copies for your friends, associates, or students without written permission. For information on using these materials for businesses, co-ops, summer camps, day camps, daycare, afterschool programs, churches, or schools please contact us for licensing.

Contact Us:

The Thinking Tree LLC

317.622.8852

FunSchoolingBooks.com   DyslexiaGames.com

info@funschooling.com

Made in the USA
Middletown, DE
11 May 2024